The INSIDE GUIDE

STEM SUPERWOMEN

Rachel Carson

By Lorraine Harrison

Cavendish Square

Published in 2026 by Cavendish Square Publishing, LLC
2544 Clinton Street Buffalo, NY 14224

Website: cavendishsq.com

Library of Congress Cataloging-in-Publication Data

Names: Harrison, Lorraine author
Title: Rachel Carson / Lorraine Harrison.
Description: Buffalo, New York : Cavendish Square Publishing, [2026] | Series: The inside guide : STEM superwomen | Includes bibliographic references and index. | Audience term: juvenile
Identifiers: LCCN 2024060039 | ISBN 9781502674685 library binding | ISBN 9781502674678 paperback | ISBN 9781502674692 ebook
Subjects: LCSH: Carson, Rachel, 1907-1964–Juvenile literature | Marine biologists–United States–Biography–Juvenile literature | Environmentalists–United States–Biography–Juvenile literature | LCGFT: Biographies
Classification: LCC QH91.3.C3 H37 2026 | DDC 508.092–dc23/eng/20250211
LC record available at https://lccn.loc.gov/2024060039

Editor: Katie Kawa
Designer: Deanna Lepovich

The photographs in this book are used by permission and through the courtesy of: Cover Everett Collection Inc/Alamy Stock Photo; p. 4 Rachel Louise Carson portrait/Wikimedia Commons; p. 6 Mihai_Andritoiu/Shutterstock.com; p. 7 Gregg Squeglia/Shutterstock.com; p. 8 Cavan-Images/Shutterstock.com; p. 9 ModernNomads/Shutterstock.com; p. 10 Rachel Carson Conducts Marine Biology Research with Bob Hines/Wikimedia Commons; p. 12 Paul Reeves Photography/Shutterstock.com; p. 13 Valentin Valkov/Shutterstock.com; p. 14 Liz Albro Photography/Shutterstock.com; p. 15 Grindstone Media Group/Shutterstock.com; p. 16 Rachel-Carson/Wikimedia Commons; p. 18 Department of the Interior/National Oceanic and Atmospheric Administration; p. 19 luchschenF/Shutterstock.com; p. 20 U.S. Fish and Wildlife Service/National Oceanic and Atmospheric Administration; p. 21 Everett Collection Historical/Alamy Stock Photo; p. 22 Rosemarie Mosteller/Shutterstock.com; p. 24 Natee K Jindakum/Shutterstock.com; p. 25 Bill Perry/Shutterstock.com; p. 26 Photodiem/Shutterstock.com; p. 27 PeopleImages.com - Yuri A/Shutterstock.com; p. 28 (top left) sjbooks/Alamy Stock Photo; p. 28 (top right) Everett Collection/Shutterstock.com; p. 28 (bottom left) Pictorial Press Ltd/Alamy Stock Photo; p. 28 (bottom right) courtesy of NASA; p. 29 (left) Nuva Frames/Shutterstock.com; p. 29 (right) PRASANNAPIX/Shutterstock.com.

CPSIA compliance information: Batch #CSCSQ26: For further information contact Cavendish Square Publishing LLC at 1-877-980-4450.

Printed in the United States of America

CONTENTS

Rachel Carson spent her life with her two great loves: nature and writing.

Chapter One

TWO GREAT LOVES

Some people love doing science experiments. Others love writing stories. Rachel Carson loved both. Growing up, she enjoyed spending time outside, studying the natural world. She also enjoyed spending time inside, reading and writing.

As Rachel grew up, those two great loves—science and writing—never changed. In fact, she found a career path that allowed her to work in both areas. By writing about the **environment**, she helped change how people understood the natural world and humans' role, or part, in it.

Exploring the Outdoors

Rachel Louise Carson was born on May 27, 1907. She grew up on a farm in Springdale, Pennsylvania, which is near the Allegheny River. The natural world was Rachel's playground as a kid. She spent hours exploring the forests and waterways around her family's farm.

> **Fast Fact**
> Rachel was the youngest of three siblings.

Rachel's mother, Maria, also loved spending time in nature. She encouraged Rachel to explore the environment around her, which was something girls at that time weren't always allowed to do.

A Young Writer

The natural world also played a part in Rachel's other favorite activity: writing. She often wrote stories about animals. When Rachel wasn't exploring nature or writing about it, she was reading books about it.

Rachel's love of reading and writing played a big part in her decision to go to college to study English. However, she eventually changed her major, or the focus of her studies, to **biology**. She graduated from the Pennsylvania College for Women in 1929 and continued her studies at

Rachel Carson spent her childhood near the Allegheny River. Today, there is a bridge named after her that crosses the Allegheny River in Pittsburgh, Pennsylvania. The Rachel Carson Bridge is shown here.

While Rachel was in college, she traveled to Woods Hole, Massachusetts (*shown here*), to study the ocean at the Marine Biological Laboratory. The ocean became a major focus of Rachel's work, including her writing.

Johns Hopkins University in Maryland. In 1932, she received her **master's degree** in zoology, which is the study of animals.

Fast Fact

When Rachel was 10 years old, she had her first story published in a children's magazine called *St. Nicholas*. Other famous writers who got their start in this magazine included F. Scott Fitzgerald, who wrote *The Great Gatsby*, and E. B. White, who wrote *Charlotte's Web* and *Stuart Little*.

Working for the Government

Rachel's first job after finishing school at Johns Hopkins University was with the U.S. government. She was hired to work for the U.S. Bureau of Fisheries, which was the part of the U.S. government in charge of fishing at the time.

THE CHESAPEAKE BAY

Rachel spent a lot of time studying the Chesapeake Bay. This is a body of water that stretches from Maryland to Virginia, with a length of almost 200 miles (322 km). The Chesapeake Bay is an estuary—a body of water that connects one or more rivers and the open ocean. In fact, it's the largest estuary in the United States.

The water in the Chesapeake Bay is known as brackish water. It's a mix of fresh water from the rivers that flow into it and salt water from the Atlantic Ocean. Many animals call the bay home, including birds, crabs, oysters, and some species of sharks.

Rachel wrote about protecting the Chesapeake Bay, which is the natural **habitat** for a wide variety of animals.

Rachel used her talents as a scientist and a writer to teach people about nature. She was hired to write radio programs about fish and other sea creatures. She also wrote for newspapers and magazines about the Chesapeake Bay and the creatures that lived in and around it.

An Aquatic Biologist

At first, Rachel only worked for the U.S. Bureau of Fisheries on a part-time basis. However, that changed in 1936. She became the second woman to be hired for a full-time job with this department.

Rachel began working as a junior aquatic biologist. This meant that she studied the living things that made their homes in the water. She also continued to write about what she studied. In fact, she was so talented as a writer that she would soon find herself working on something much bigger than the **pamphlets** and radio programs she created for the government.

Fast Fact

An aquatic biologist is like a marine biologist. However, marine biologists generally focus their work on things that live in the ocean, and aquatic biologists often focus more on freshwater creatures. This isn't a **strict** rule, though, and aquatic biologists sometimes study sea creatures too.

Today, the U.S. government employs many women as aquatic and marine biologists. That's a big change from Rachel's early days with the Bureau of Fisheries.

Rachel found a way to combine her knowledge of STEM—science, technology, engineering, and math—with her skills as a writer. She's shown here with the famous wildlife artist Bob Hines.

STORYTELLING WITH SCIENCE

Chapter Two

Rachel had been using her skills as a writer since she started her career with the U.S. Bureau of Fisheries. However, things changed in a big way for her in 1941. That year, her first book was published. This led to a new chapter in her life, in which she combined storytelling and science in a way that made many people care about the environment more deeply than they had before.

Rachel's First Book

When Rachel first started working for the U.S. government, she wrote an essay, or a piece of informative writing, called "The World of Waters." Her boss thought it was very good—so good, in fact, that he told her it should be published in something bigger than a government pamphlet. In 1937, it was published in a magazine called *The Atlantic* with the new title "Undersea."

A major publishing company wanted Rachel to turn her essay into a book. She did this, and in 1941, *Under the Sea-Wind* was published.

Fast Fact

The U.S. Bureau of Fisheries became part of the U.S. Fish and Wildlife Service soon after Rachel started working for the department.

In *Under the Sea-Wind*, Rachel used different animals, such as the sanderling (*shown here*), to tell the story of life in and around the ocean. Her creative writing helped people emotionally connect with scientific facts.

Fast Fact

Under the Sea-Wind didn't sell a lot of copies when it was first published. However, it's now considered one of the most important books about nature ever written in the United States.

This book presented scientific facts about the sea through the stories of different sea creatures.

A Big Success

Rachel's next book told a big story, and it became a big success. She wanted to give readers the full history of the ocean, but she first needed to do a lot of research. She met with oceanographers—people who study the science of the ocean—and learned about the latest technology used to explore the sea.

Rachel's hard work paid off. In 1951, *The Sea Around Us* was published, and it became a bestseller. In fact, people loved this book so much that they wanted more of Rachel's writing. They discovered *Under the Sea-Wind* and made that book a bestseller too!

Fast Fact

In 1952, *The Sea Around Us* won a National Book Award. This is a prize given to the best books written by Americans each year.

The Story of the Shore

Rachel had written a lot about the ocean, but now she wanted to tell the story of the shore. Rachel studied the coast, learning about the

Some people call *The Sea Around Us* the biography, or life story, of the ocean. Once again, Rachel's beautiful writing helped people understand and care about science in a new way.

A NEW PATH

Rachel worked for the U.S. government until 1952. She stayed with the U.S. Fish and Wildlife Service for her entire government career, writing many different educational materials for this department. She eventually became the editor in chief in charge of all the writing that was done for the U.S. Fish and Wildlife Service.

Rachel's 15-year career ended when she left her position with the government to focus on writing books. The success of *The Sea Around Us* gave her enough money to follow this new path.

land and the **organisms** that called it home. She used this research to write *The Edge of the Sea,* which was published in 1955 and became another success.

In *The Edge of the Sea,* Rachel described coastal environments as their own system of living things that were connected to each other. This

Rachel was interested in ecology, or the science of how living things interact with the natural world around them. In *The Edge of the Sea*, she helped people understand ecology by describing life along the seashore.

was the first time many readers were introduced to the concept of an ecosystem.

Moving to Maryland

In 1957, Rachel's life changed in a big way that had nothing to do with writing. Her niece died, leaving behind a young son named Roger. Rachel decided to adopt the little boy, and she moved with him to Silver Spring, Maryland. She built a life with him there while also taking care of her mother.

After moving to Silver Spring, Rachel became very interested in the effects of pesticides on the environment. These chemicals were meant to kill harmful bugs, but many of them also hurt other living things too. Rachel knew people had to be warned about this before things got worse.

Rachel began studying the effects of pesticide use in the 1940s. She believed the spraying of these chemicals over large areas of land could harm entire ecosystems.

Rachel's fourth book, *Silent Spring*, helped average Americans understand why they needed to care about the environment. Because of this, many people say it helped start the modern environmental movement.

Chapter Three

SILENT SPRING

Rachel put her talents for scientific research and writing to use once again as she tackled the tough topic of pesticide use in the United States. She knew that important groups—especially the chemical companies that made pesticides—wouldn't like what she was writing. However, she knew she had to tell the truth about what was happening to the environment. The natural world needed someone to speak for it—before it went silent forever.

Research and Writing

Rachel's pesticide research focused on one chemical in particular, which was known as DDT. She talked to other scientists, attended government hearings about pesticides, and spent years gathering her own facts about the ways DDT was already harming the environment and could harm it even more in the future.

> **Fast Fact**
>
> Rachel didn't want to write *Silent Spring* at first. She'd hoped someone else would take on the pesticide companies. However, she wrote, "Knowing what I do, there would be no future peace for me if I kept silent."

Rachel's research came together in a finished product

Silent Spring **got its title from the idea that DDT was killing the birds that sang in the springtime.**

in 1962. First, a magazine called *The New Yorker* published a serialized **version** of *Silent Spring*, which meant it was broken up into smaller sections—like episodes that come together to make a TV series. Then, *Silent Spring* came out as a book.

What Rachel Wrote

In *Silent Spring*, Rachel wrote about the many ways DDT was harming ecosystems. She stated that the use of this pesticide was hurting more than just the pests it was supposed to kill. One of the groups of animals most affected by DDT was birds.

Fast Fact

Rachel wrote that scientists had classified, or named, DDT as a carcinogen. This is a kind of substance that is known to cause cancer.

One reason for this was the fact that DDT didn't break down easily, so it stayed in the bodies of animals that

WHAT IS DDT?

DDT was first used to kill bugs during World War II (1939-1945). This was very helpful at the time, because bugs were spreading sicknesses that were killing soldiers and **civilians**.

By the end of the war, DDT was approved for use by the public in the United States. The U.S. government supported its use because DDT killed bugs that could harm the food supply, so its use allowed farmers to grow more crops to feed a booming population. However, the publication of *Silent Spring* made people aware of the dangers of DDT, and today, it's only used in **developing** countries that need it to kill disease-spreading insects.

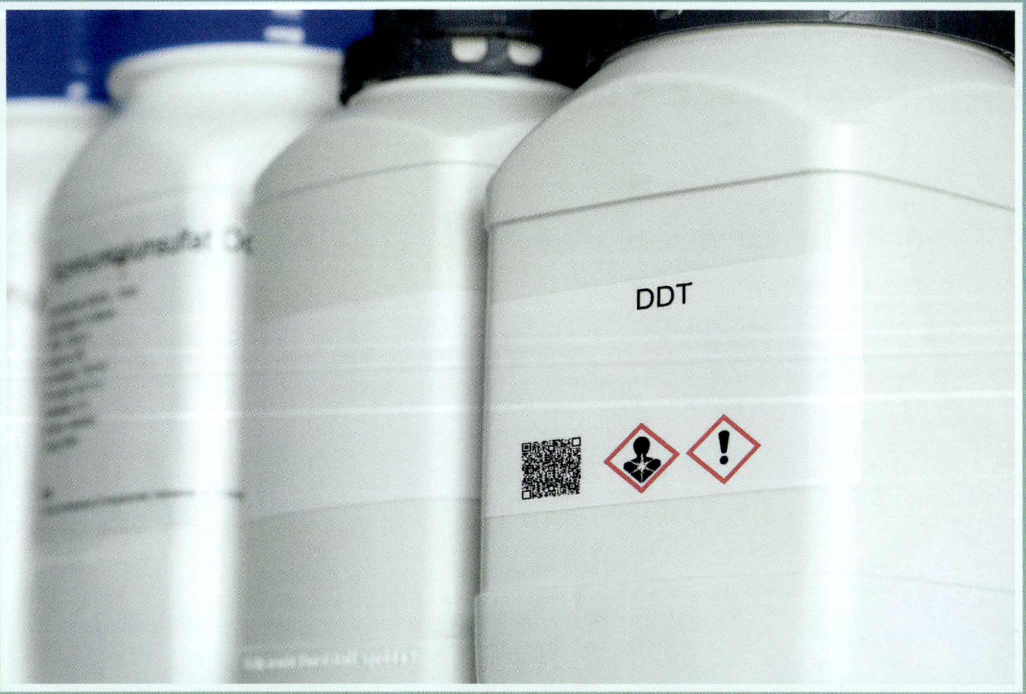

DDT is the shortened name of the chemical dichlorodiphenyltrichloroethane.

were exposed to it. It then moved up the food chain, especially when birds ate the insects that were exposed to it.

A New Perspective

Silent Spring opened people's eyes to the negative effects humans could have on the environment. At the time, many people believed that humans were meant to control the natural world. They didn't care about the effects scientific progress or new technology had on other living things.

After reading Rachel's words, however, many people began to think more about the environmental consequences of human progress. Rachel gave them a new perspective, or way of seeing things.

Critics and Supporters

Rachel knew *Silent Spring* would make some people angry, and she was right. The chemical companies that produced pesticides tried

Rachel didn't call for a ban on pesticides. She knew they had a purpose. However, she supported more careful use of these chemicals and a better understanding of how they affected the natural world.

Fast Fact

On April 3, 1963, a TV special called "The Silent Spring of Rachel Carson" aired on CBS—one of the major television channels at that time. Millions of Americans watched Rachel read from her book and talk about her research.

to discredit her, or say she wasn't to be trusted. Many of them tried to argue that because she was a woman, she was too emotional to be trusted with scientific facts.

Actual scientists, however, supported Rachel's work. In fact, a special committee put in place by President John F. Kennedy validated, or agreed with, the research Rachel presented in *Silent Spring*. This led to major changes in how the U.S. government viewed and used pesticides.

John F. Kennedy was the U.S. president when *Silent Spring* was published. Rachel testified, or spoke, to his Science Advisory Committee about the effects of pesticides on the environment. She also spoke about this issue in front of the U.S. Congress.

Statues of Rachel Carson, such as this one in Woods Hole, Massachusetts, honor this scientist and writer who laid the foundation for the environmental movement as we know it today.

THE START OF A MOVEMENT

Chapter Four

Silent Spring changed the way many people—including U.S. government leaders—viewed and treated the natural world. Rachel's words helped people understand that humans play a part in their ecosystem just like any other living thing, and she showed people that we weren't always playing the part of the hero.

Rachel didn't live to see the full impact of work, though. She died not long after *Silent Spring* was published.

A Long Battle

While Rachel was writing *Silent Spring,* she found out she had breast cancer. She had surgery and went through different kinds of treatments, including **radiation** treatments, but she chose to keep her

Fast Fact

The radiation treatments Rachel went through existed because of the work of another female scientist—Marie Curie. In the late 1800s and early 1900s, Marie experimented with radiation and how it could be used to treat cancer.

The Sense of Wonder deals with the importance of introducing children to the wonders of the natural world.

illness private. She was worried that the chemical companies would say it made her less credible, or trustworthy.

Rachel kept getting sicker, even as she testified before government groups and appeared on CBS. She died on April 14, 1964. The next year, an essay that Rachel had been working on was published as a book titled *The Sense of Wonder*.

Major Changes

Rachel was gone, but she lived on in her words, which inspired important actions by many groups, including the U.S. government. After the release of *Silent Spring*, the government began reviewing its use of pesticides, especially DDT. A decade later, the general use of DDT was banned in the United States.

Fast Fact

The EPA was created by U.S. president Richard Nixon.

The EPA has been called "the extended shadow of *Silent Spring*."

Rachel's words also played a part in the creation of a new government agency. In 1970, the Environmental Protection Agency (EPA) was created to address environmental problems, such as the ones Rachel wrote about in *Silent Spring*.

The Environmental Movement

Rachel's work didn't just have an impact on how the government treated the environment. It also changed how average Americans viewed their role in the natural world. Rachel's ability to present scientific facts in an emotional way helped ordinary people understand that our actions have consequences for the environment. This led to a new desire to protect the natural world, which grew into the modern environmental movement.

WOMEN IN ENVIRONMENTAL SCIENCE

In many ways, Rachel's work laid the foundation for the modern study of environmental science, which is the branch of science that deals with humans' impact on the environment. Environmental scientists use different STEM skills to address environmental problems.

Many women have made their mark in this field. They include Nzambi Matee, an engineer from Kenya who is working to turn plastic waste into building materials, and Dr. Katharine Hayhoe, a scientist who is educating people about the effects of climate change. Today, groups are working to encourage even more women to become involved in environmental science and other areas of STEM.

The number of women in environmental science is small compared to the number of men in the field. This is because women and girls aren't always encouraged to pursue careers in STEM. Organizations are working to change this and support girls and women who are interested in STEM.

Today's environmental activists, who speak out about the ways humans continue to harm the natural world, are following in Rachel's footsteps.

Words Can Change the World

Rachel Carson spent her life bringing together the two worlds she grew up in—the natural world and the world of words. Her work shows us that STEM and writing can come together to move people and create change.

Rachel once wrote, "In nature nothing exists alone." By teaching us that everything in the natural world is connected, she changed how we think about the environment and our place in it. Rachel Carson's words changed the world, and they continue to inspire us today.

Fast Fact

The Rachel Carson Wildlife Refuge—a protected ecosystem—is located in Maine.

According to Rachel Carson, every living thing has its own part to play in nature. We can play our part by keeping the natural world around us clean and safe for other living things.

TIMELINE

In Rachel's Life

1907
Rachel Louise Carson is born in Pennsylvania on May 27.

1936
Rachel begins working full-time for the U.S. Bureau of Fisheries, where she would work for the next 15 years.

1941-1955
Rachel writes a trilogy, or set of three books, about the ocean: *Under the Sea-Wind*, *The Sea Around Us*, and *The Edge of the Sea*.

1962
Silent Spring, Rachel's most famous work, is published.

1964
Rachel dies on April 14.

World Events

1903
The first World Series is held to determine the champion of Major League Baseball.

1929
The Great Depression begins, hurting economies around the world and leaving many without work.

1939-1945
World War II is fought.

1963
Dr. Martin Luther King Jr. delivers his "I Have a Dream" speech.

1969
U.S. astronauts become the first people to walk on the moon.

THINK ABOUT IT!

1. How did Rachel's childhood interests shape her life as an adult? Do you have any interests now that you think will shape your life in the future?
2. Why do you think *Silent Spring* made such an impact on the public and the U.S. government?
3. What do you think Rachel would write about if she was still alive today?
4. What are some ways we can help protect the environment?

GLOSSARY

biology: The branch of science that deals with living things.

cancer: A sometimes deadly sickness in which cells grow in a way they should not, often forming tumors, or growths, that harm the body.

civilian: A person not on active duty in the military.

developing: Having few industries and many people who are unable to buy the things they need.

environment: The natural world around us.

habitat: The natural home for plants, animals, and other living things.

master's degree: A title given to students following additional years of study at a college or university after receiving their bachelor's degree, which is generally given after four years of study.

organism: An individual living thing.

pamphlet: A short printed publication with no cover or with a paper cover.

radiation: Waves of energy.

strict: Absolute, kept with great care.

version: A form of something that is different from others.

FIND OUT MORE

Books

Croy, Anita. *Rachel Carson*. St. Catharines, ON: Crabtree Publishing Company, 2021.

Dalal, Anita. *Investigating Nature: Women Who Led the Way*. New York, NY: Children's Press, 2022.

Rooney, Anne. *Rachel Carson*. New York, NY: Franklin Watts, 2020.

Websites

Engaging with the Environment: Women's History
www.nps.gov/subjects/womenshistory/engaging-with-the-environment.htm
The U.S. National Park Service provides an overview of how women have worked with the environment throughout history, including links to stories about famous female environmentalists.

National Women's History Museum: Rachel Carson
www.womenshistory.org/education-resources/biographies/rachel-carson
The National Women's History Museum presents a short biography of Rachel Carson, along with links to biographies of other groundbreaking women.

Rachel Carson Council
rachelcarsoncouncil.org/
This organization was founded to carry on Rachel's environmental work after her death.

Publisher's note to educators and parents: Our editors have carefully reviewed these websites to ensure that they are suitable for students. Many websites change frequently, however, and we cannot guarantee that a site's future contents will continue to meet our high standards of quality and educational value. Be advised that students should be closely supervised whenever they access the internet.

INDEX